Playtime

Lunchtime

Bathtime

ne

How you can help

Understanding the concept of time and learning to tell the time are big steps in any child's life. **First steps with ladybird** *time* looks at the idea of time, using colourful illustrations to tell the story of a brother and sister's day, from getting up in the morning to going to bed at night. Each of the familiar scenes is related to the time on a clock face.

- Enjoy talking about the illustrations together. What is Sally doing in this picture? What do you do first in the morning – eat breakfast or get dressed? The little mouse echoes the actions and provides lots of opportunities for talking and laughing.

There are lots of other ways you can help your child to learn about time. Look out for different clocks at home or outdoors. Enjoy talking about the day's events, using words like before, after, etc. Counting rhymes, songs and games like 'What's the time, Mr Wolf?' will help, too.

Ladybird would like to thank Priscilla Hannaford, freelance editor on this series.

A catalogue record for this book is available from the British Library

Published by Ladybird Books Ltd
80 Strand London WC2R 0RL
A Penguin Company

10 9

© LADYBIRD BOOKS LTD MM

time

by Lesley Clark
illustrated by Peter Stevenson

Ladybird

It's 7 o'clock.

GOOD MORNING!

It's daytime and Sally and
Billy are wide-awake.

What do they do first?

Talk with your child about the order in which he does things in the morning. What does he do first?

It's 8 o'clock.

They have a wash.

I'm quite quick at washing...

Which things can your child do quickly? Which things does he do a little more slowly?

It's 9 o'clock.

What do Billy and Sally do *next*?

It's 10 o'clock.

What do *you* do in the mornings?

It's 11 o'clock.

Sally is having a drink.

It's 12 o'clock and it's the middle of the day.

My *tummy-rumbles* are telling me *it's* time to eat.

It takes a long time to get it ready but a short time to eat it!

It's 1 o'clock.

GOOD AFTERNOON!

Billy and Carla are having a race.

It's 2 o'clock.

Billy helps Mum to hang the washing out to dry.

Can we pick up Sally now?

In an hour.

What do you do in the afternoon?

Look at the time!
It's 3 o'clock.

Time to collect Sally from school.

Talk about how clocks are useful for reminding us when to do something and how long we have to do it.

It's 4 o'clock.

Look at the pictures of
Sally and Billy baking a cake.

What do they do first?

It's 5 o'clock.

GOOD EVENING!

It's getting late.

Everyone is hungry.

Who's already got an empty plate?

It's 6 o'clock.

It's bathtime.

"I've had my bath. I'm ready for bed."

Now it's Sally's turn to have a bath.

It's 7 o'clock.

It's night-time.

Time for Sally to go to bed.

Come on Sleepyhead,
it's not time to play.

At night it's dark.

What things happen while you're asleep?

Talk about what happens in your child's night and day.

Look at clocks throughout the day.
When do you eat, bath and play?

7 o'clock   8 o'clock   9 o'clock

2 o'clock   3 o'clock   4 o'clock

10 o'clock   11 o'clock   12 o'clock   1 o'clock

5 o'clock   6 o'clock   7 o'clock

What a busy week!

On Monday Billy goes to playgroup.

On Tuesday he stays with Gran.

On Wednesday Carla comes to play.

On Thursday Billy goes to the shops.

On Friday Billy and Carla go for a swim.

On Saturday Billy plays with Sally.

And on Sunday he helps his dad.

Keep a weekly record of regular activities, and paint or cut out pictures to help your child remember the sequence.

first steps with ladybird

First steps with ladybird is a range of mini readers, activity books and flash cards designed to develop the essential early skills of children aged 2 and upwards.

Mini readers

These durable hardback books use photographs and illustrations to introduce important early learning concepts.

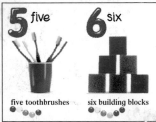

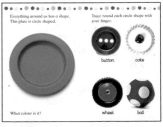